#OUCH!

Sold Out at The New York International Fringe Festival!

"This comedy of errors puts in perspective why our health system is in dire need of repair. And that's no joke."
—Peter Riegert, actor/host of *Vocal Heroes* podcast

"A major win...brutally honest...riotously funny...deeply insightful...I can't recommend it enough!"
—Jeff Messer, *880therevolution*

What doesn't kill you makes you stronger...or crazy...or both. *#OUCH! (An Accidental Comedy)* is a hilarious account of one woman's adventure in the modern American health care system. From the moment her dog leaves her broken in the mud, it's a wild ride. At the mercy of policemen who legally can't touch her and EMTs who legally can drug her, she winds up in trauma surgery at a hospital where a mystery rash is sweeping the wards. Between the missionary housekeeper who insists she come to Jesus and the giggling nurses who sneak snaps of her derriere, this true story would be a tragedy if it wasn't so ludicrous. Once she finally makes it home, she must deal with imminent financial ruin because her insurance company denies her existence. The absurdity never ends. That's what makes *#OUCH!* both funny and frightening. A multimedia tour de force for a solo performer, this one-act is a sidesplitting romp through a tangle of red tape.

Also published by The Sublime Theater & Press

American Arcade
by Steven Samuels

My Crazy My Love
by John Crutchfield

Washington Place
by David Brendan Hopes

#OUCH!
An Accidental Comedy

MARYEDITH BURRELL

THE SUBLIME THEATER & PRESS
Asheville, NC

#OUCH! (An Accidental Comedy)
Copyight © 2021 by Maryedith Burrell

Published by The Sublime Theater & Press, Inc.
49 Faircrest Road, Asheville, NC 28804-1848
ss@thesublimetheater.org

The Sublime Theater & Press, Inc. is a 501(c)(3) tax-exempt organization.

All rights reserved. Except for brief passages quoted in newspaper, magazine, radio, television, or online reviews, no part of this book may be reproduced in any form or by any means, electronic or mechanical, including photocopying or recording, or by an information storage and retrieval system, without permission in writing from the publisher.

Professionals and amateurs are hereby warned that this material, being fully protected under the Copyright Laws of the United States of America and all other countries of the Berne and Universal Copyright Conventions, is subject to a royalty. All rights including, but not limited to, professional, amateur, recording, motion picture, recitation, lecturing, public reading, radio and television broadcasting, online presentation, and the rights of translation into foreign languages, are expressly reserved. Particular emphasis is placed on the question of readings and all uses of this book by educational institutions. Inquiries concerning production rights for or any use of any kind of this play should be addressed to the publisher.

ISBN 978-1-952720-09-3 (Hardcover)
ISBN 978-1-952720-10-9 (Paperback)
ISBN 978-1-952720-11-6 (E-book)

First edition, November 2021

#OUCH! (An Accidental Comedy) was first presented by The Magnetic Theatre in a workshop performance at Asheville Community Theatre's 35below, 35 East Walnut Street, Asheville, NC, May 14, 2014.

The world premiere was presented by The Magnetic Theatre at The BeBe Theatre, 20 Commerce Street, Asheville, NC, October 2-12, 2014.

The production was revived by The Magnetic Theatre at Magnetic 375, 375 Depot Street, Asheville, NC, May 22-24, 2015.

Subsequently, the production was presented by The Magnetic Theatre in The New York International Fringe Festival on the 64E4 Mainstage, 64 East 4th Street, New York, NY, August 21-29, 2015.

Written and Performed by Maryedith Burrell
Produced and Directed by Steven Samuels
Visual, Scenic, and Sound Design by Tommy Calloway
Lighting Design by Abby Auman (BeBe and Magnetic 375)

#OUCH! (An Accidental Comedy) is a one-person show. Inspired by true events in the life of the original writer/performer, the play works for any gender. It is written with aside passages, interaction with media, and frequent use of a "Sidebar."

STAGE DIRECTIONS: Not optional. They are choreography that is integral to the meaning of the play and essential to the comedic beats.

TEXT REVISIONS: Updating data regarding U.S. medical costs may be necessary to insure accuracy. No other text revisions are allowed.

THE SIDEBAR: Downstage right, it consists of a small bar and barstool, and is designated with a classic neon martini gobo. It is literally where informational "sidebars" to the topic are addressed as well as where the actor can take a short time-out. All props at the Sidebar (water, grapes, mirror, makeup, towel, etc.) are used to refresh in real time. The Sidebar is a separate reality both physically and emotionally.

MEDIA: Refers to original production design elements projected on an upstage screen. Graphics, slides, cartoon animation, data, etc., should be timed for comic effect and/or be easily read by the audience. The "Accidental Death & Dismemberment" office is designated by a slide.

SFX: Refers to music or audio cues.

PROPS: All are handheld and moved by the actor throughout the play. The Desk is assembled with black multipurpose cubes. The Shrine is also black and should look like a typical Catholic kneeler with a small votive candle tray and cross. At The Shrine are The Mantilla, TheraBands, and small Hand Weights. The Sidebar and Sidebar Stool are also black. All Sidebar props should be on the bar. The Rolling Office Chair is black, with multidirectional wheels that move silently and smoothly over the stage floor per the action.

#OUCH!
An Accidental Comedy

Preset media: "#OUCH!" title slide.
Lights out. Slide out. Lights up on...
A WOMAN, black mantilla on her head, deep in prayer, kneeling at a small shrine.
MEDIA: "Mater Dolorosa" (Virgin Mary icon with seven swords piercing her heart).
SFX: "Salve Regina" sung by a choir of angels.
The Woman becomes aware of the audience.

WOMAN: Oh, there you are. Glad you could make it. Hang on just a second, I'll be right with you.

(Removes her veil, picks up two hand weights and does an arm exercise routine during the following)

Thank you all for coming. Did you find decent parking? Ushers treat you right? Good. Sorry, but I've got to do this, hope you don't mind. Not enough hours in the day. Got to work on that poster body. Truth in advertising, right? You see, I had an accident about a year ago playing fetch in the park with my dog, Miss Butters.

(Pointing to the screen)

Now referred to as "The Perp."

(SFX: Law & Order cell door slam/echo. MEDIA: "BUTTERS a.k.a. 'The Perp'"—scruffy mutt incognito in Ray Ban sunglasses)

Mommy still loves her Fluffy-Butt-Rescue-Dog-From-Outer-Space. Mommy just can't run like the wind anymore.

(Switches to arms overhead)

It was an accident. Accidents, like shit, happen. But I was in Asheville, North Carolina: the Alternative-New Age-Microbrewery-Bee-Tattoo-Smoky Blue Buckle on the Bright Red Bible Belt.

(MEDIA—Asheville, NC images: Mellow Mushroom restaurant, Green Man Brewery, tattoo parlor, CBD vape shop, 12 Bones BBQ, Billy Graham Highway sign, Women's March bare-breasted lesbians, Black Lives Matter art on Lexington Avenue, etc.)

A unique community complete with Biltmore, the Vanderbilt mansion turned Downton Abbey Petting Zoo, and a charming town where wealthy retirees, gender benders and closet Proud Boys synchronize swim and pretend they don't see the unvaccinated kid peeing in the shallow end. So things got weird pretty fast.

(Does a triceps exercise)

Let me be clear. I moved to Asheville of my own free will. And I have nothing against the AARP, pansexuals or "Paul's Letter to the Ephesians." But I think we can all agree that Asheville is where the Patchouli and Preachers collide, so I got a lot of conflicting response to my accident. Everything from "I'm flying you to the Mayo Clinic to see a real doctor" to "Honey, this is the universe asking why your significant other is another species."

(Finishes weights, grabs a TheraBand, wraps it under her right foot, holds it in one hand and flexes her foot up and down with resistance)

Metatarsals, phalanges: you want pain-free flexibility and good tracking in both feet. You want to be able to actually *feel* your feet. Nerves take a long time to come back—if ever.

(Switches to the other foot)

So, yeah, I love my friends. Couldn't get through a day without them. But when your right leg looks like the Goodyear Blimp and a fireman is cutting you out of your jeans, there is no time to fly to Florida. And you don't want your manicurist quoting *A Course in Miracles*. When your dog knocks you down like a 16-pound Brunswick at Sky Bowl, it's too late for amethyst geodes and nettle infusions. You want sirens and Schedule II narcotics. But I get ahead of myself. I forgot to tell you about The Police.

(Gets down on the floor with the TheraBand and does a series of leg raises)

I couldn't get up. I literally could not pull myself out of the mud. I thought I twisted my knee, so I got hold of my friend Chris...

(MEDIA—tweet: "Shitfuckhelp@#ouch!")

But she couldn't help me up without causing agony, so she called the police. Two of Asheville's finest showed up, but they couldn't touch me. They could not legally lift me or handle my person in any way as long as my leg was attached to my body. I kid you not. If my leg was dangling and looked all *Game of Thrones* or if it was actually severed, they could find it in the bushes, throw me over their shoulder and take me to the nearest hospital. But as long as my leg was just swelling up like a poisoned horse and I wasn't screaming "I want to kill myself," the police could not touch me. This I found surreal, maybe because by this time I was in a kind of shock.

(MEDIA: sci-fi shock victim. Woman sits up, faces audience)

It's now about a half hour into my accident. I'm sitting in mud in a park, and I've made several calls on my cell phone. I think I've just twisted my knee, so, being Type A, I'm organizing everything. I've made an appointment at the "Emergency Walk-In" at an orthopedist's office. I have found a couple of Advils at the bottom of my purse covered in lint and I have swallowed them dry. I'm crazed, and I'm arguing with two policemen who can throw me on the ground and take my drugs but cannot pick me up and give me an aspirin. *(Pause)* So we all agree to call the Fire Department.

(Does the other leg with the TheraBand)

Ladies and Gays, I'm with you when it comes to Firemen. They are fabulous! They work out all day waiting for bells to ring so they can save people. They cook, they clean, they do their own laundry. And, if TV can be believed, they're all smokin' hot in the sack and no longer wear those silly Tom Selleck mustaches. Firemen are, in a word, "Heroes."

(Wraps her leg up in the TheraBand)

The firemen who came to save me were almost kind of just like that. Well, one was almost sort of just kind of like that. The one who examined my leg like Willoughby in Jane Austin's *Sense and Sensibility.*

(Ties the TheraBand off in a neat bow)

But how many firemen does it take to lift a gal out of the mud? FIVE. Two to actually do it, one to get a leg brace off the truck, one to keep asking me if I want an ambulance, and another to fill out paperwork with the policemen who can't touch me.

(Struggles to raise herself up off the ground in her TheraBand "brace")

Now let me be clear. I was in a ton of pain, so I could be fuzzy on some of this. I'm sure everyone was just doing their duty. I know Chris got my dog in *my* car and the firemen got me into *her* car and off I went to the Emergency Walk-In...

(Hops over and sits in a rolling chair, leg extended out straight)

...where I was met with a wheelchair, and they X-rayed me and told me that I was mistaken. I did not have a twisted knee. I had a *tibial plateau fracture*!

(MEDIA—X-ray: tibial plateau fracture)

And where nobody would give me an aspirin or a Dilaudid despite the fact I was a patient with a popular football injury and somewhere they call "Emergency Walk-In." And where they told me that I would need surgery and I promptly burst into tears.

(Reflects for a moment)

My crying seemed to upset my doctor. This I found odd since he is in the broken-bone business. I mean he must deal with men, women and children, old, young and in-between in various stages of pain and agony every day. It's common knowledge that when you break a bone it hurts, and the idea of surgery isn't very pleasant either. So when I got the bad news I cried buckets. And that's when my doctor slowly backed away from me...and told me to go home and wait until Monday.

(Scoots the chair slightly forward each time she says "wait until Monday")

Go home and wait until Monday...for my swelling to go down.

Wait until Monday...so I could interview one of their surgeons and schedule an operation for maybe Wednesday or Thursday. I should go home with my broken leg and wait until Monday... It was Friday.

(Stops the chair, rises casually, and points to a small bar stage left. On it are a small makeup mirror and makeup, water, some fresh grapes, Kleenex, a small hand fan and towel, etc.)

Sidebar?

(Lights—gobo: "SIDEBAR". SFX: ice clinking in a glass; lounge music. Woman sits on the barstool, drinks)

Like many people on the planet, I currently live alone. I have a little three-story house with an attic office and my bedroom is on the second floor.

(MEDIA: three-story LEGO house)

I do not have servants or a chauffeur or family nearby to make sure I take my medication or to cook me a tuna noodle casserole. The surgery I need is not elective, it is what is called *"traumatic."* So, I am fucked. My doctor isn't asking me where I live or how I live. He's offering to send me home with some Oxy. So I guess he thinks I'll be taken care of like Michael Jackson...

(MEDIA: Michael Jackson in famous military jacket)

...and the concierge physician I have on retainer will shoot me up with Propofol so I can sleep for three days. Then, when I wake up on Monday, my staff will dress me like The Nutcracker and carry me back to "Emergency Walk-In" where the best surgeon east of the Mississippi will of course agree to operate on me immediately.

(Rises from the bar, back in leg brace mode)

So now I'm not only crazed with pain, I'm panicking. My leg is the size of a small child, it hurts like hell, and my doctor isn't making any sense. I can't wait until Monday. I can't walk and I'm freaking out!

(MEDIA—pain and suffering montage: Saint Sebastian; naked Indian ascetic with weights on genitals; sleazy law ad for damages and "Pain & Suffering"; injured dancers and athletes)

They say that can happen with pain…freaking out. There is physical pain, there is emotional pain, "suffering" usually comes with it. Lawyers get money for "pain and suffering." How we do or do not endure pain seems to be some kind of test of character in western culture. Are you brave or are you a big baby? Girls can cry, boys can't. Being able to take pain comes with practice—like dancers and athletes and soldiers. Soldiers suffer for their country. Saints suffer for Jesus. I was raised Catholic; we canonize people who inflict pain on themselves to identify with the Passion of Christ.

(MEDIA: The Passion of Christ *poster)*

A lot of people saw that Mel Gibson movie and *Son of God* too. I am not one of those people. I would fall into the Big Baby category. I come from a long line of Big Babies. Oh, but I forgot to tell you about my gene pool.

(MEDIA—film posters: Sid & Nancy, Lassie, Patton, The Nun's Story, Spartacus, Dallas Buyers Club*)*

We're no strangers to addiction, judgment and rebellion. My

people are not what you would call stoic. We bitch, we moan. We feel every pea under every mattress. I personally avoid pain whenever possible. I don't like pain. I don't find it ennobling. I'm not convinced that "what doesn't kill you makes you stronger" either. I think it can really screw you up for life. I've seen people get depressed and sadistic with too much pain. So, when the "Emergency Walk-In" doctor suggested I go home on my broken leg and wait until Monday—without asking what my home looked like or if I had anybody to take care of me—you can see that I was not genetically equipped for that kind of test.

(MEDIA: Lone Survivor *poster; James Franco in* 127 Hours *sawing off his arm)*

Do I look like some Special Forces guy? James Franco trapped under a boulder? No. I am a woman of a certain age in Asheville, North Carolina, and on that Friday afternoon I was experiencing more pain than I'd ever known in my life and I was just trying to get a little help. Sidebar.

(Makes for the bar and sits. SFX: lounge music; ice in glass. She pours a shot of water, throws it back, then turns to the audience)

It's true, I am a woman, but I've never given birth. I've been a birth coach so I know what real pain *sounds* like, but I've never had contractions myself. I lived in L.A. but I was never shot in a drive-by either, but I bet it hurts. And until my accident I'd never broken anything substantial in my body that required surgery. I've thrown a motorcycle a few times, fallen out of a tree, been kicked by a Rockette and the neighborhood bully ran over my face with his bicycle when I was nine—all of which was very painful—but nothing came close to the pain I was feeling in that doctor's office on that Friday. And I didn't care how many prescriptions he gave me, there wasn't enough heroin in Hamburg to get me to Monday.

(Rises, adopts a courtroom attitude)

At this time I would like to give a shout-out to the nurses of the world. Were it not for a lone nurse at this critical juncture in my orthopedic adventure, I would never have known what my options were. I would never have understood that I could demand an ambulance at any time. And I would not have known that it was the only way I could get any morphine and I would never have met my new best friends, Carlos and Dave.

(MEDIA: two smiling, buff EMTs. SFX: ambulance siren!)

Anybody ever been in an ambulance?!

(Grabs the rolling chair, drives it around stage like an ambulance dodging set pieces, whipping past the first row, etc.)

It is so cool!!! It's like a My Little Pony hospital. Everything you need for any kind of emergency—heart attack, flaming car crash—it's all there and engineered by anal retentive Japanese toy makers. The people that brought you "Princess Luna" made the "Friendship Is Magic Neonatal Blood Pressure Cuffs" and the "Pinky Pie Defibrillators." And all of it is magically stored in tiny cubicles and mini-drawers. Plus the pharmacy is always open! So praise the Lord and pass the PIIC *[pronounced "pick"]* line, Blue Cross is buying!

(Plops down in chair center stage, grabs the TheraBand, ties off arm)

You know EMTs are even better than firemen, because instead of hoses they have narcotics. And Carlos and Dave were the best. They tag-teamed me onto that gurney like Lady Gaga Dancers. They put me out of my misery pronto. Those boys heard me when I said: "Baby needs to ride the dragon!"

> *(Drugged to the gills, she spins around in her chair. SFX: "Volver, Volver" by Los Lobos. After a couple of spins, she stops, tries hard to focus)*

I am a cheap date. I hardly drink, barely smoke pot. Half my family are Irish alcoholics and the other half are mean, backsliding Presbyterians. So I rarely indulge because my relatives made for a very chaotic childhood. But one of the best things about my accident was the fact that the morphine was guilt-free. And I'm sure you'll agree that there is no better time than when you break your skeleton and you're on your way to a hospital to get high. Who'd want to go there straight? Hospitals are like bad Sheratons. They're cold, they're beige, they're transreal. You're paying to be a science experiment, and between the sleep deprivation and the MRSA viruses all over the place, you would never go there unless you were high as a kite. *(Giggles)* Sidebar?

> *(Rises cautiously, heads for the bar. SFX: ice in glass; lounge music. The minute she reaches the bar, she's stone cold sober)*

Excuse me, but at this point in the show I need a little air.

> *(Uses the electric fan to cool off—face, neck, hairline, armpits)*

It's hot up here. And, quite frankly, reliving these memories takes a lot out of a girl…I mean woman…I mean carbon-based life form, child of God, whatever.

(Drinks water, towels off. Adjusts seat and sits)

At this time I think it's important for you to know who I was when I had my accident. The "before" if you will. You know they say your life flashes before you like a movie when you think you're dying, so you should know what was going on in my drug-addled brain as I sped off in that ambulance to the emergency room. I was sure that life as I knew it was over. My days of being hip and happening, gone. It was the end of an era. Because you see this was me BEFORE the accident:

(MEDIA: Jimmy Choo red suede and diamond high heels)

I was all girl, all the time. I went places, I did things. I was the kind of gal that threw a pair of jeans and a little black dress in a bag with some hot stilettos and headed off to London. So, you see, in that doctor's office on that tragic Friday, I wasn't just crying because my leg was broken and I needed surgery. No. I was crying because Jimmy Choo had left the building. Because I knew this was my future:

(MEDIA: beige Birkenstocks)

Ladies, I know you feel me. Gentlemen, I'm sure you can relate. It takes a real man to refuse Rogaine. So, there I was speeding off to the Emergency Room, drugged out of my mind, facing the indignity of spending the next month naked in a hospital gown depending on the kindness of strangers, and I was having real trouble clinging to my identity. All I knew for sure was that sirens were wailing and I was heading straight into a crucible.

(Rises, sets the rolling chair center stage)

The staff at my hospital seemed to have a sixth sense for when I was having visitors. Exactly two minutes before friends arrived a nurse would slip me a bedpan.

(Places an imaginary bedpan on the chair, sits awkwardly and tries to get comfortable)

Like Marie Antoinette *"en toilette,"* people would come and go while I sat on that thing. Very humiliating. The third time it happened, a housekeeper came in to mop the floor and asked me if I had a personal relationship with Jesus. There I am trying to do my business and she's telling me Jesus can heal my leg and right my bowels. No moment was too awkward for this woman and her scatological theology. Now normally when Jehovah's Witnesses or Mormons ring my doorbell I am able to be gracious, to understand that they, like The Blues Brothers, believe they are on a mission from God. I can take a pamphlet, smile and send them on their way. But after surgery, high on morphine and sitting on a bedpan—I went off on the bitch. I told her The Nazarene and I were in couple's therapy and she'd be bathed in more than the Blood of the Lamb if she didn't get the hell out of my room!

(MEDIA—therapy scene: Male therapist with Blue-Eyed White Jesus head and female patient with the Woman's head)

But I forgot… *(Lost)* Oh, yeah… *(Lost again)* You know memory is a tricky thing.

(Goes downstage right, confides in an audience member)

I don't remember arriving at the hospital. I do remember my friend Chris being in the Emergency Room with my purse and telling me my dog was safe at home with sitters. I remember being in a corridor and somebody named Wendy wanting to know if I had a Medical Power of Attorney and I told her I was just fine to fill out a clipboard full of legalese—and she let me! I was tripping. I probably signed my house over to QAnon.

(MEDIA: "QANON HEADQUARTERS" sign on LEGO house)

Then I was in a hospital room where I stayed for a really long time, then a really short time, and somebody named "Calamari" had his name on a chalkboard and he told me I had a clean break and didn't need surgery. Then Batman and Robin came in and told me that I did. Then my friend Steve made it okay.

(Crossing stage left to another group)

You know Steve says I sang a duet with him in surgery prep. I don't remember any of that, but I do remember insulting my trauma surgeon. I told him I didn't want some doctor they just "scraped off a golf course" cutting me open. I have since apologized. But what could I do? I was like a dog at the vet.

(SFX: heart monitor getting louder and louder. Scared, she grabs the rolling chair, sits)

Everything smelled anonymous. My mojo was at an all-time low. I was Crazy Horse in jail—trapped, spirit broken, surrounded by people who didn't understand me. And there wasn't a downer on the planet that could tame my Lizard Brain. Nothing was going to make it okay for strangers to break my protective seal and cut me open. It was fight or flight time.

(MEDIA: exit sign)

I saw my chance! My surgeon was telling Steve it was time to go. An exit sign was glowing up ahead. I struggled to rise from my gurney, it was now or never...

(Rises, fighting the drugs and desperate to get away, when she is stopped abruptly by a golden light. MEDIA—miracle: the operating room is overcome by light; out of the glow emerges a young George Clooney as Dr. Doug Ross in ER*)*

Then a miracle happened! George Clooney took my hand and said, "Good morning Maryedith, I am your anesthesiologist!"

(SFX: Lawrence Welk's "Colorado Sunset." She turns "blushing debutante"; waltzes with her imaginary Dr. Clooney, reciting the following as she covers the entire stage)

They tell me I had surgery on Saturday morning and it lasted three hours. They say they put steel rods and a steel plate in my leg. Nobody asked if I wanted titanium. I was so out of it I probably would have insisted on platinum and asked school children to write a poem on my plate. That way, if I ever got scanned at an airport, I could be fashion-forward and bring a message of peace and hope to people making $17,000 a year looking for terrorists. *(Dizzy)* Sidebar anyone?

(Floats to the bar; the waltz fantasy drops immediately. SFX: "Colorado Sunset" abruptly ends; ice in glass; lounge music. She addresses the audience while she checks her makeup in the mirror, uses the fan to cool down, etc.)

Don't let anybody fool you. Surgery changes your life. Oh, you'll dance again if you practice every day...but you must practice every day. The once-pristine vessel that was your perfect body has been cut, clamped, and modified and you will never be the same. You know, it's one thing to plan a hip replacement, it's quite another to be playing in the park and 24 hours later you and The

Golden Gate Bridge have a lot in common.

(MEDIA: post-surgery X-ray with steel rods and a shot of the Golden Gate Bridge. She rises, stands like a medical model)

It was hard to wrap my brain around. I was Random Theory incarnate.

(Checks for audience confusion, offers an explanation)

I know some of you may think Random Theory and Chaos Theory are one and the same. They are not as you can plainly see.

(Turns to the screen. MEDIA: Random Theory/Chaos Theory jumble of math. She waits for an "ah-hah" moment that never comes, proceeds)

So there I was, felled by a random act of cosmic mischief, a classic Trauma Patient, and thanks to our American health care system, it took about six months and $70,000 to fix. And that's just the skin and bone. What about the "trauma?" The PTSD of it all?

(Goes into soap opera mode. SFX: dramatic music stings punctuate the following)

Nobody at the hospital or in rehab ever talked about that!
(Sting)
About the shock of my life being turned upside down,
(Sting)
losing months of work,
(Sting)
having a scrambled brain,
(Sting)
the stress of worrying about money and coordinating aftercare.

(Organ arpeggio)
I never got so much as a pamphlet!

(Plops down into the rolling chair. SFX: self-pity violin)

Oh, there was physical therapy and occupational therapy—how to use crutches, how to bend over and pick up a book I couldn't read. And that's stuff you need to know if you're in a thigh-high brace hopping around on one foot for four months. But unless I asked the perfect question and bugged people until I got an answer that made sense to me, nobody offered any advice on a full mind/body recovery. Nobody talked about depression, stress, adrenal failure…unhealthy weight gain.

(SFX: Gothic organ sting. She flies backward in the rolling chair, slapping frantically at her body. She catches herself, stops, takes a much-needed deep breath)

Nobody ever asked me what I did for a living. Nobody ever asked what "back to normal" meant to me.

(Leaps up, places the chair center stage like a ballet barre. Does a ballet drill throughout the following)

The fact I wasn't a 20-year-old ballerina seemed to make it okay for 60% mobility in my leg after the first go-round of physical therapy. I had to argue for more. I write and teach for a living so I needed to be able to think, to read, to concentrate, and if I couldn't, it was legitimate cause for concern. Nobody could tell me why I was having trouble reading a magazine. *(Pause)* They were leg people. *(Pause)* I was gaining weight like crazy, but nobody brought up cortisol levels or suggested I up the B vitamins and protein in my diet. And on top of that, my trauma surgeon had one afternoon a week for follow-ups. That meant a mob scene in reception and didn't leave much time for anything but "Hey, your scar looks great." So I was left to wonder: What would Ida Rolf do? Where could I get some acupuncture? Maybe a little soma? And how come I know body work helps reintegrate things and my doctor won't discuss it?

(Gets stuck down in a "grand plié")

Oh, but I forgot to tell you about my insurance company!

(MEDIA: tsunami about to swallow a patient. She gestures to the bar)

Shall we?

(Straightens up effortlessly, goes to the bar and pours water into a martini glass. SFX: ice in glass; lounge music)

Like I said, I'm not a 20-year-old ballerina so I had to be a squeaky wheel just to get some physical therapy. And I'm not 95 and out of it either, so my insurance company hated me.

(Adding a twist of lemon to her glass)

They don't like people who remember things.

(Adjusts herself on the stool and carries on)

Trying to get paid was a hassle and a hassle at a time when hassling is counterproductive to the healing process. Thank god I wasn't recovering from a heart attack or battling cancer because I had to fight my insurance company every day. No lie. And I don't think my experience was unique. I think it was typical—and that's what really pisses me off.

(Sets her glass back on the bar, goes stage right, talks to the audience)

Dealing with Major Medical and Aftercare insurance was a nightmare, and a nightmare I wasn't prepared for because I'm average. The average person doesn't have "Insurance Drills" four times a year. We don't practice calling our Claims Adjuster or pretend we're having a stroke one day or an appendectomy the next. I had a good plan through my union and I had the foresight to get an extended care policy a few years back, so I thought I was covered. And I was. What I wasn't covered for was the year-long bureaucratic shitstorm I had to go through to get paid!

(SFX: Thunder! Lightning! Mussorgsky's "Night on Bald Mountain." MEDIA—Bureaucratic Shitstorm: Wizard of Oz *tornado; Butters is the Wicked Witch on a broomstick; Carlos and Dave are blown away in their ambulance; paperwork swirls everywhere, forming a giant mountain. Woman takes cover behind the rolling chair. When the storm dies down, she peeks out)*

I could build a yurt with all the computer-generated mail I got. *(Sitting)* I stressed over billing errors, collection agencies that were notified prematurely, the right-hand zombies who wouldn't talk to the left-hand zombies, the east coast offices that wouldn't talk to the west coast offices, insurance officers who wouldn't talk to doctors, doctors who filled out forms wrong, lost forms, copies of forms, copies for everyone of the form that was lost that I copied before. Did I mention my office was in the attic? My life was all about super bills, getting to know gals in offices, who was an idiot, who was sharp, who was awake in what time zone. I learned a lot about how modern insurance conglomerates interface with hospitals and pharmaceutical companies. Doctors seemed to be the least of my worries.

(Remembers something, blushes)

Oh, I'm sorry, I forgot to tell you about my hookup.

(Turns "Marilyn Monroe." Grabs the rolling chair, drags it like a mink stole across the floor, sits, spins, flirts with the audience)

I had an aftercare policy that was supposed to kick in the minute I got home, but I ended up having to dip into my savings to pay for ramps, rides and caregivers. I waited three weeks to get an evaluation, another two months to get my first check. According to the doctor, I couldn't walk or drive or do anything for at least four months, but the insurance company danced with the idea that somehow I was going to bathe myself and fry my own eggs high on Oxy and balancing on one foot. And they were just baffled by the fact my policy was generated in California and I was now living in North Carolina. The delays got so bad I consulted a lawyer who started throwing around words like "deliberate negligence" and "fraud." Three months into my home care, after much squeaking, I got a call from the Vice President of Claims begging me not to sue or go to the press. He blamed everything on new computers. Well, I told him "I just had surgery and I can't figure out Photoshop on my Mac but I still manage to pay my premium!" At which point I think he got it—I was a single woman and I wasn't going anywhere. I couldn't walk, I couldn't drive, I couldn't work. I had a lawyer…and I now had his phone number! He was trapped, he was desperate…so he asked me out.

(Breaks character, motions to the bar)

Nice guy, a little pedantic, which brings me to Obamacare. Sidebar?

(SFX: ice in glass; lounge music. She goes to the bar, munches

on a bunch of grapes, offers some to the audience)

Whether you're a fan of The Affordable Care Act or you think it's a slippery slope, there is a reason everybody needs insurance. Hospitals in America cost way too much. And who is asking why?

(MEDIA—magazine covers: including Time's *"Bitter Pill," by Steve Brill)*

Mr. Steve Brill for one. His *Time* article came out while I was in orthopedic rehab. So there I am trying to heal on mac and cheese and rice pudding, watching *Law & Order* on a continuous loop, and I finally get a nurse who will read a magazine to me and it's Steve Brill all about how I'm being ripped off and health care in this country isn't a free market—especially when you're in an accident. And the nurse does not like what she's reading at all. She tells me Mr. Brill must be a Commie and the American health care system is the best in the world so I shouldn't worry my pretty little head about anything... Then she tries to give me Codeine I'm allergic to.

(Pours a glass of water, drinks)

I swear it's like the whole country has Stockholm Syndrome. We're in love with our captors. We think nonprofit hospitals aren't in it for the money. We think insurance companies want to pay us. And we think we can eat at McDonald's as much as we want and still look good in white jeans. Sorry, no. And all the noise about how we're going to pay the bills just distracts from the real problem—the bills.

(Rises, goes center stage. MEDIA: The Soap's Journey)

Think about it. Instead of refusing to pay $50 for a bar of soap in a hospital, we line up every year and pay billions to a middleman who has convinced us that he is the only one who can negotiate with that hospital and get us a bar of soap for just 20 bucks. A bar of soap that costs 50 cents wholesale. Who ate their firstborn and cursed us with this madness?

(MEDIA: U.S. Congress)

Insurance companies have been lobbying the U.S. government for 250 years with very good results. It all started in the 1700s with "Assurance" companies—as in "I assure you your widow will get paid." And as the cult of The Doctor grew over the years along with science and technology, American medicine got a fine reputation for being cutting edge and everybody was more than happy to pay through the nose for the best. After all, it's life and death, and you get what you pay for, right?... Or do we?

(MEDIA—malpractice headlines: drug recalls; FDA scandals; V.A. hospital atrocities)

My friend Phyllis went all the way to New Delhi for a hip replacement. She said the personal care she received over there blew her mind. Her own doctor in L.A. acknowledged that her procedure was state-of-the-art and the device they gave her in India was higher quality than what she would have gotten in the U.S. on her insurance plan. He was happy with her rehab report too. Her meals were high quality and specifically designed to reduce inflammation and promote healing. She had the same two nurses throughout her stay. Her doctors visited her constantly and she had physical therapy every day for eight weeks. All included—plane tickets, surgery and her aftercare cost one third of what it would have cost her in America. She came home and wrote a book about it.

(Sets the rolling chair center stage)

It's always been a statistics game, insurance. Companies and clients gambling against catastrophe. But now the concept of "too big to fail" has entered the picture. So what happens to somebody "too small to succeed" in a world like that?

(Stacks two boxes in front of the chair to create a desk)

When I got out of college I signed up with a temporary employment agency and they sent me to an insurance company in Los Angeles. I was told I was hired because I was cute and I could type. They put me in the Accidental Death & Dismemberment Department...

(MEDIA: "ACCIDENTAL DEATH & DISMEMBERMENT DEPT." logo)

...where the supervisor was packing for a Hawaiian vacation. He did not train me in any way. Instead, a secretary sat me at a desk piled high with giant binders. She called them "actuarial tables" and said they listed how much an accident was worth. My job was to answer the phone, listen to what the policy holder had to say, find their injury on one of the tables, tell them how much money they were getting, then fill out a requisition slip for that amount. Oh, and a white injury was worth more than a black one back then... Just saying.

(Turns into a twenty-year-old, sitting nervously at her desk, checking out the office and people around her. SFX: phone rings once, twice... She finally realizes the phone is ringing for her and answers)

Hello?... I mean, "Accidental Death & Dismemberment Department"... Yes, Mrs. Henderson...

(Listening to story)

The whole right arm?... A thresher, that's farm equipment, right?... No, I've never harvested wheat personally, but I can imagine it's difficult without your right arm... Okay, do you mind if I put you on hold for just a minute?... Thank you, Mrs. Henderson.

(Reaching for a binder, flipping through pages)

Midwest...right arm...white male...58...thresher...

(Confused, picks up the phone)

Pardon me, ma'am, but did you say your husband's arm was mangled or missing?... Yes, well, a bit mangled is a blessing isn't it?... Okay, here we go. *(Reading)* You are entitled to receive $1800.

(Wincing, holds phone away from ear)

That's what... I'm afraid that's what the chart says... Well, I'm terribly sorry for your situation and...

(The line goes dead)

Mrs. Henderson? Mrs. Henderson?

(Rises, addresses the audience)

I couldn't sleep at all that night. The next day I was asked to make coffee for everyone on my floor and to man the phone once again.

(SFX: phone. She stares at it, afraid to answer. Finally, she breaks down and lifts the receiver)

Accidental Death & Dismemberment... Yes, Mr. Sanchez, this is the right desk... How many? Three toes?... No, I can see how that could happen with a John Deere lawn mower... Sir? Sir, excuse me, but if you are bleeding... Yes, well a tourniquet and ice is a good idea, but you should really go to a hospital... Pardon me?... Yes, I've heard of World War II... D-Day, yes... Seriously, Mr. Sanchez, if it's that bad you really should call an ambulance... Oh, you've got your toes in a baggie with ice and your daughter's on her way from work... If you don't mind my asking Mr. Sanchez, how old are you? Eighty-two last week, well happy birthday. And you say you live in Arizona, alright...

(Looks it up)

Lawn mower...three toes...self-inflicted... That will be *(Incredulous)* $925. That doesn't sound right. $925 a toe maybe...

(Off Mr. Sanchez)

I know, wait a minute please.

(Gets a notepad and pen and starts making notes)

You said you've had your policy for how long? Forty years!

(Making sure nobody can hear her)

And you're over 80 and a war veteran, right?... What I mean is, I think we may have some wiggle room here... *(Calculating)* If we allow for inflation...and shipping and handling...loss of blood and of course all the ice... Mr. Sanchez, I think I can put in a requisition for $9,250. How's that?... My pleasure... No, thank you for your service, sir... Is that your daughter I hear? Good. You take care now... Don't forget your toes... 'Bye.

(Looks sheepishly around the office. Nobody's paying any attention to her so she relaxes and puts her feet up on the desk. SFX: phone)

Accidental Death & Dismemberment.

(Holding the phone from ear)

Yes, I can hear you Mr. Eberly... Factory hearing loss? Oh, you know I don't think we...sure why not?

(Yelling into receiver)

I said WE COVER THAT... No, workman's comp won't be a problem... Where are you?... WHERE DO YOU LIVE, SIR?... Detroit!...

(Checking a binder)

Mr. Eberly, by any chance are you African American?... ARE YOU BLACK?...

(Closing the binder)

Well, congratulations... CONGRATULATIONS! We just lifted the red line in your neighborhood and you're getting $14,000 with an option for more... I SAID YOU'RE GETTING A BIG CHECK!... No, thank you, Mr. Eberly.

(Hangs up and rises from the desk)

Nobody questioned any of my requisitions, so the following day I called back Mrs. Henderson in Indiana and told her that I was new and I had made a terrible mistake. Instead of $1800, she and her husband would be getting $18,000 plus physical therapy. I quit before the supervisor got back. In total, I think I gave away about $150,000 in ten days and I never heard a peep from anybody. It was my last insurance job and my first foray into the world of philanthropy.

(Breaks down the desk and resets the stage during the following)

So, karmically speaking, maybe I deserved the hassle I got from my aftercare company. Maybe waiting months to get paid was my punishment for committing insurance fraud right out of college. But I know I made some deserving people happy. I know the company I worked for never trained me or bothered to check my performance. The people in the office were more concerned with how I made coffee than how much money I was giving away. Insurance companies aren't Too Big To Fail. I think they've been slipshod for awhile. Too Big To Care maybe… Oh, but I forgot to tell you about the Channel 4 News.

(MEDIA: Asheville Channel 4 News Team)

I'd like to share one final story. There are lots—like the time the caregiver was so feeble she dropped me in the tub. The time I went to the rehab beauty parlor with the Alzheimer patients. You haven't lived until you've had your roots done with two ladies who think they're in Tudor England. A lot of crazy stuff happened, but I think this one pretty much says it all.

(Balances on her left side horizontally on the rolling chair, with her right leg going up and down in an imaginary leg-motion machine)

I had surgery on a Saturday. By Sunday morning I had a bad itch in a very awkward place. Now I'm high on morphine, I'm in a hospital bed, my leg is strapped to a motion machine and my right butt cheek feels like I've got poison ivy. I call for the nurse, she comes in, takes a look, then says "Hang on" and leaves the room. She returns awhile later with a younger nurse who takes one look at the spot, giggles, and asks me if I've "seen the news." She tells me there is a "mystery rash" going around the hospital and it's been all over local TV.

(Stops moving)

Now I know what you're thinking. You're thinking these nurses can't help themselves. They were obviously dropped on their heads at birth. Because giggling and asking if I've seen the news is just so wrong on so many levels: 1) I am an orthopedic surgery patient not their BFF at Forever 21; 2) I just got out of surgery, and, you know, they don't let you bring your cell phone in there so I couldn't get the tweet from Nurse Betty telling me how cool it is my hospital is on TV; and 3) What hospital staff in their right mind is happy about a "mystery rash" outbreak?!

(Starts moving her leg again)

So I've just woken up from surgery, my leg's going up and down and it hurts, there's a mystery rash in my hospital and on me, and all anybody wants to do is "take a look." There's a constant stream of people—nurses, assistants—who want to "take a look." All day and all night they're "taking a look." Nobody's culturing my rash to get a diagnosis, nobody's telling me what it is, and I'm itching like crazy and I can't take it anymore. So I finally grab somebody and suggest that the mystery rash might be some kind of herpes and maybe a tube of Zovirax cream could do the trick.

(Stops moving)

A few hours later I get a call from Accounting. They need preauthorization because a tube of Zovirax is going to cost me one thousand dollars. *(Pause)* I kid you not. One thousand dollars for a two-inch tube you can get at CVS for three dollars with insurance. I know because I called CVS delirious from my hospital bed. So, I declined. I declined everything. I declined the thousand-dollar itch cream. I declined everybody "taking a look." I declined all the giggling and the pointing. And I declined the nurse who wanted to snap a picture of my rash on her iPhone for some dermatologist I never met. I told her if I saw my ass on Reddit I'd sue her, the hospital and everybody in it.

(Sits up straight, faces the audience)

There was a doctor in my room ten minutes later. He had some cream that didn't cost one thousand dollars. I asked him what my rash was, and he said he didn't know, but other people got relief from the cream so he was going to try it on me. Like I said, we willfully donate our living tissue to strangers and hospitals are transreal.

(MEDIA—Butters in shades with transrealist books: Philip K Dick's A Scanner Darkly; *Margaret Atwood's* The Handmaid's Tale; *Rudy Rucker's "A Transrealist Manifesto"; etc. Woman moves center stage)*

The day I left for orthopedic rehab the missionary housekeeper I threatened with my bedpan came back to clean my room. I apologized for going off on her and she said she understood. I was in a lot of pain and it's hard to hear the Word of The Lord when the devil's in your veins. That was such a great way to put it. "Pain is a devil in your veins." Leg pain, trauma pain, corporate bullshit pain—it's all a devil in our veins. And there's another devil we don't like to talk about: the devil that says a 500% profit is great but a 2000% profit is better. Exactly how much profit is enough when it comes to human misery?

(MEDIA: transreal Butters riding a rocket up rising health care costs)

According to *The New York Times*, the U.S. has an annual health care bill of about three trillion dollars. That's more than the Gross Domestic Product of France. I know we have more people than they do, but that's a lot of defibrillators and Vicodin. And how are you and I supposed to deal with a massive system like that without going crazy or bankrupt or both? We're busy, we're distracted, we're standing in lines for iPhones. I get it. One thing I learned from my accident was that I needed to be proactive.

(Walks down center)

I suggest Insurance Drills.

(Pointing to audience member)

Don't laugh. I'm serious. You don't want to be trying to read the fine print in your policy when you're on drugs, trust me. I did it and it wasn't pretty. Drink a double latte and read your policies cover-to-cover when you're sober.

(MEDIA—montage: Woman drinking coffee at Starbucks and on her cell phone, and reading Insurance Policy; tour guide and Woman with other tourists out in front of a modern hospital; Woman shaking hands with a hospital social worker; Woman giving cookies to gals in hospital accounting)

Get a point person at your company and their direct line. They have to talk to you in person. If they won't, get a better company that will. Know your hospital before you need it. Very important. Go over there and find out what their infection rate is. They have to disclose it by law. And say hello to the Social Worker. Every hospital has one. They know how the place really works and they are there specifically to help you. Then, go down to the cubicles and talk to the gals in accounting. Bring them some cookies; those are the ladies you're really going to need. Because...

(Gets her mantilla. SFX: "Salve Regina" up low. MEDIA: "Mater Dolorosa" fades in)

Chances are we're all going to experience some pain in this life. And if believing Jesus has your back makes it better for you, amen. If a doctor can take your pain away, call him *[Spanish pronunciation]* "Jesus." If a fireman comes to your rescue, give him a medal. And if a nurse hears you and cuts through all the red tape, give her a set of wings.

(Puts the mantilla on her head, kneels down at the shrine)

And if you live to tell the story, light a candle for a friend.

(Turns on a flameless votive and bows head in prayer. Lights slowly fade. SFX: "Salve Regina" rises, then is suddenly cut off by a record scratch. Lights flicker. So does the "Mater Dolorosa." Lights pop up full again)

I forgot to tell you about the special flippers!

Lights out. MEDIA: "#OUCH!" slide. SFX: "Heart of Steel" by Galactic.

ABOUT THE AUTHOR

Maryedith Burrell has turned her diverse talents into an award-winning career. Her numerous writer/performer credits include everything from *Fridays* and the iconic *Seinfeld* to *The Tonight Show* and an overall deal with Disney to create original TV and film. A classically trained thespian and playwright, she derailed into improv comedy with The Groundings and Second City, and voiced the adult animation series *Duckman*. Her latest documentary, *RAISE HELL: The Life And Times of Molly Ivins*, won raves at Sundance 2019 and SXSW, and is now streaming on Hulu. *#OUCH! (An Accidental Comedy)* premiered at The Magnetic Theatre in Asheville, NC, and was cited by *The New York Times* as a Top 10 "must see" at the New York International Fringe Festival. Ms. Burrell is an adjunct professor of Stage & Screen at Western Carolina University, a member of Flatiron Writers, and currently lives in the Great Smoky Mountains of North Carolina. (For more information, visit maryedithburrell.com.)

www.ingramcontent.com/pod-product-compliance
Lightning Source LLC
Chambersburg PA
CBHW030142100526
44592CB00011B/1006